Private Law 2.0:
On The Role of Private Actors in a Post-National Society

Private Law 2.0:
On The Role of Private Actors in a Post-National Society

Inaugural lecture delivered by

Jan M. Smits

as Maastricht-HiiL Chair on the Internationalisation of Law

on Tuesday 30 November 2010

eleven
international publishing

Published, sold and distributed by Eleven International Publishing
P.O. Box 85576
2508 CG The Hague
The Netherlands
Tel.: +31 70 33 070 33
Fax: +31 70 33 070 30
Website: www.elevenpub.com

Eleven International Publishing is an imprint of Boom uitgevers Den Haag.

ISBN 978-94-90947-17-0

Esteemed Rector Magnificus and Dean
of the Faculty of Law,
Dear members of The Hague Institute on
the Internationalisation of Law,
Dear students and colleagues,[1]

Prologue

This inaugural lecture marks the beginning of my activities on the Maastricht-Hiil Chair on the Internationalisation of Law. It is not the first inaugural lecture that I give. I had the pleasure of addressing a different audience earlier this year at Tilburg University,[2] and ten years ago I stood at this very same place here in Maastricht.[3] With a variation on Oscar Wilde, one is tempted to say that to leave one university may be regarded as a misfortune, but to leave a second one looks like carelessness. I am all the more delighted that you have come to listen to me, and I can reassure you that I do not plan to give a fourth inaugural.

The title of this lecture may strike you as ambitious. The term 'Private Law 2.0' seems to suggest that our present-day private law is no longer fit for purpose and therefore needs to change. This suggestion is right. I will argue today that the time has come for nothing less than a change of paradigm in the way we think about law – not only about private law, but also about several of the other traditional legal sub-disciplines. All I ask from you in the coming forty minutes is to follow the argument I try to make, and then to tell me at the reception whether you are convinced by it or not. I am a fierce believer in the point that I will make this afternoon and I can already say now that I plan to continue to make this point in the coming years.

1 This text largely reproduces the original spoken version of the lecture. However, some parts were elaborated and footnotes were added to ease access to the materials on which this lecture is based.

2 *Rechtstoerisme: Burgerlijk Wetboek en Grondwet voorbij de Staat*, Tilburg University 2010.

3 *The Good Samaritan in European Private Law: on the Perils of Principles without a Programme and a Programme for the Future*, Maastricht University 2000.

Samantha and the Law

My plea consists of three consecutive steps. In the first step, I would like to introduce you to a fictitious person. Let us call her Samantha. Samantha has three aims in life: to happily marry the person she loves, to earn money with her own company and finally, to own a nice holiday house in a sunny country. We can infer from these desires that Samantha is not an anti-globalist. We will not find her in Toronto or Seoul protesting against a meeting of the WTO or the G-20. However, it is safe to say that her aims in life are not unique. In fact these are aims shared by many other people throughout the world. These are desires about shaping one's life in the way one wants to do this (both personally and professionally), so about getting married, about setting up a company and about buying a house abroad. What Samantha needs to achieve these goals is law, more specifically private law. Private law offers the framework for private action: it facilitates choice by people like Samantha. At the same time, private law not only facilitates choice, it also sets the limits for it.

An important question that is dealt with by lawyers on a daily basis is who sets these rules for private action. Where is it that Samantha should look for the rights and obligations that govern her life? The prevailing paradigm in private law is that we still find most of the relevant rules in Samantha's 'own' national law. In case she would live in a civil law jurisdiction, like The Netherlands, the presumption is that these rules are laid down primarily in the Dutch Civil Code and in the case law of the highest court. If she would live in a common law jurisdiction, like England, it would be presumed that it is the national case law, next to statutes, that primarily sets her rights and obligations.

I hasten to add that everyone today would accept that we also have rules coming from outside one's own country – like the rules of European law. And yet, there is a gap between the formal recognition that this is the case and the way in which we look at law, present law and teach law to students. One only needs to have a look at the Dutch textbooks (or, in fact, at the textbooks of any country) to immediately recognise that only one source of private law is presented as really important. In civil law jurisdictions, textbooks therefore tend to follow the structure and the contents of the Civil Code. Another example of the central role of national law is offered by the formal policy of the Dutch Ministry of Security and Justice to implement all European elements as much as possible into the Dutch Civil Code in order to maintain the coherence of the national legal system.[4] If we follow this prevailing view, Samantha can be happy: she only needs to look into the Dutch Code, some case law and statutes (or read a textbook) to find out what are her main rights and obligations. And we may not immediately realise this, but this is part of a paradigm (a view underlying the theories and methodology on a particular subject). It is the paradigm of a State monopoly in setting the rights and obligations of people. This paradigm finds its origins in the Peace of Westphalia of 1648. It is the idea of a State having exclusive control over a territory and over its people. The general picture is that it was only with the Peace of Westphalia that the existing 'chaotic void'[5] of facts, politics and religion was slowly filled by the 'real' law of the sovereign states. State sovereignty thus became the fundamental ordering principle, making the law shift not only from fragmentation to coherence, but also from plural to monolithic.

I will now take a few minutes to confront this prevailing view with reality. Is it really true that Samantha can learn about her main rights and obligations by looking into her own national law? My reading of today's society is that she cannot. The conduct of today's citizens is in my view even surprisingly little governed by national law. I mention four phenomena that are perhaps well known separately, but that are rarely taken together.[6]

4 Handelingen EK 1 March 2005, *EK* 17-759 ff.

5 A. Claire Cutler, *Private Power and Global Authority: Transnational Merchant Law in the Global Political Economy*, Cambridge 2003, 244.

6 See in more detail Jan M. Smits, The Complexity of Transnational Law: Coherence and Fragmentation of Private Law, in: *Netherlands Reports to the Eighteenth International Congress of Comparative Law* (Washington 2010), Antwerpen-Oxford 2010, 113 ff.

Four Phenomena

7 Cf. Daniela Caruso, Private law and State-making in the Age of Globalization, *New York University Journal of International Law and Politics* 39 (2006), 1 ff.

8 Jan Smits, Europese integratie in het vermogensrecht: een pleidooi voor keuzevrijheid, preadvies NJV 2006, in: *Handelingen Nederlandse Juristen-Vereniging* 136 (2006-1), 57 ff.

9 Gunther Teubner, Breaking Frames: The Global Interplay of Legal and Social Systems, *American Journal of Comparative Law* 45 (1997), 149 ff., at 157.

First of all, there is the rise of new centres of institutional power.[7] The best-known example of this is the rise of the European Union as a lawgiver. As is the case in any of the legal fields, private law increasingly flows from the European legislature and courts. I once calculated that more than 10% of the provisions of the Dutch Code are derived directly from implemented European directives.[8] However, this implementation at the national level does not mean that we no longer need to look at the European directive itself. When the national judge interprets the implemented law, it should look at the aim of the directive, the case law of the Court of Justice of the European Union, and preferably also at how national courts in *other* countries have dealt with the directive. But this is not all. Talking about centres of institutional power beyond the nation-state, we also have an increasing number of decisions of human rights courts and rules issued by the WTO, the IMF and the World Bank with a direct impact on how private parties should conduct themselves in matters of free trade, taxes, intellectual property and protection of health. These rules are supplemented by well-known international conventions, like the Convention on Contracts for the International Sale of Goods (CISG), and by the rise of executive agencies of, in particular, the European Union that also make decisions that are of direct relevance to private parties.

Secondly, there is an increasing amount of what my predecessor on this Chair, Gunther Teubner, has called 'private global norm-production'.[9] With this term, Teubner refers to codes of conduct for corporate social or environmental responsibility, to rules of standardisation organisations for technical standards (such as the 'codex alimentarius') and to other types of self-regulation including, in contract law, the age-old standardised general conditions. Samantha's business life is in reality much more influenced by these rules than by national law. Still a different type of voluntary law consists of the sets of academic soft law that have emerged in the last decade. The best-known example is the Draft Common Frame of Reference of European Private Law[10] that has as a primary aim to influence the setting and interpretation of norms by the European lawmaker.

It is important to realise that most of these authoritative rules and norms would not be recognised as binding in a traditional conception of law: they do not meet the formal requirement of being enacted by the relevant authorities. However, in reality they do set the norms for specific groups of people and are therefore important in predicting their behaviour. Grainne De Burca rightly qualifies this phenomenon as the emergence of 'authoritative rules, norms and policies from sites of governance beyond the nation-state'.[11] In the same vein, our German colleagues Nils Jansen and Ralf Michaels speak of 'private law beyond the State'.[12] And the American author Larry Backer persuasively demonstrates how influential such norms can be: he shows that in particular large multinational companies are able to create their own systems of rules and can impose these upon their suppliers and customers. These self-contained autonomous systems of global law are, in his view, as powerful systems of customary law as the early English common law was in its day.[13]

There are still two other reasons for the now rapidly decreasing importance of national law – reasons that do not have to do with new types of norms, but with the changing conduct of citizens themselves. The first thing to mention here is that private actors are increasingly mobile: the essence of the globalisation process is that citizens travel abroad and companies do business on the other side of the border, leading to a truly global interconnectedness. There is probably little need to convince you of this phenomenon, but I do want to spell out that, as a result of this process, the rights and obligations of people like Samantha are also in this respect often no longer dependent on their

10 Christian Von Bar & Eric Clive (eds.), *Principles, Definitions and Model Rules of European Private Law: Draft Common Frame of Reference*, München 2009.

11 Grainne De Burca, Developing Democracy Beyond the State, *Columbia Journal of Transnational Law* 46 (2009), 101 ff., at 104.

12 Ralf Michaels & Nils Jansen, Private Law Beyond the State? Europeanization, Globalization, Privatization, *American Journal of Comparative Law* 54 (2006), 843 and Nils Jansen & Ralf Michaels, Private Law and the State, *Rabels Zeitschrift* 71 (2007), 345; also see the special issue of *American Journal of Comparative Law* 56 (2008), 527.

13 Larry Catá Backer, Economic Globalization and the Rise of Efficient Systems of Global Private Law Making: Wal-Mart as Global Legislator, *Connecticut Law Review* 39 (2007), 1739 ff.

'own' national law: buying a house in Italy prompts the need to look into Italian law and buying things over the internet may also have legal consequences that were never anticipated. In many cases, it is not the law of the supplier of the goods that is made applicable in such contracts, but (for example) the law of Luxembourg.

The fourth and final phenomenon to point at, is that it increasingly happens that people choose another law than that of their 'own.' Not only can people travel, also the law can travel. When Samantha is building up her company, she can make all kinds of strategic decisions motivated by what law she likes best. She can, for example, choose to incorporate her company as a Limited under English law whilst concluding contracts with her business partners in Italy and Sweden by making German law applicable to these contracts. If Samantha is an Italian living in Italy, wanting to marry her Polish girlfriend, she can do so by concluding a same sex marriage in Canada. It may be that this marriage is not recognised in all of its aspects in her state of residence, but there is no doubt that Samantha is able to marry and take this qualification with her when she returns home.[14] Earlier this year, I paid attention to this phenomenon of, what I call, 'legal tourism'.[15] I then tried to show that this is no longer something in the margin, but an essential part of today's law: private actors increasingly consider law no longer as something by which they are governed, but as something they can govern themselves. Apparently, people are not always happy with the entire package of law of their residence or nationality and therefore decide to 'opt out' of one or more specific aspects of their legal system.

This phenomenon is now high on the academic agenda. Some academics have recently described it in terms of a 'law market'[16]: similar to how a consumer can buy the food that she prefers at a supermarket, one can shop for the law to one's liking. It means that law, at

14 This is not possible in every country that allows same-sex marriage: most of these countries set strict requirements of residence or of nationality to avoid 'marriage tourism.' Thus, in Dutch law one of the partners must be either a Dutch citizen or a legal resident of the Netherlands. This is different in Canada, South Africa and Mexico City. It does therefore not come as a surprise that Canadian statistics show that among the marriages concluded between same-sex couples in Canada, more than half are in fact between foreigners not living in Canada itself. See the marriage statistics of Statistics Canada, available at www.statcan.gc.ca and K. Harris, Same-sex marriage drawing foreigners, *CNews* 18 January 2007.

15 Jan Smits, *Rechtstoerisme: Burgerlijk Wetboek en Grondwet voorbij de Staat*, Tilburg University 2010. The theoretical foundations for this view of people not voting through parliaments, but with their feet, were laid by Charles Tiebout, A Pure Theory of Local Expenditures, *Journal of Political Economy* 64 (1956), 416 ff.

16 Erin O'Hara & Larry E. Ribstein, *The Law Market*, Oxford 2009; cf. Horst Eidenmüller, Recht als Product, *Juristen-Zeitung* 64 (2009), 641 ff.

least in those areas where such a law market is allowed to exist, is becoming a product. And to show you how right this view of law as a product actually is, even in the perspective of national States, it suffices to point at some recent documents. First, there is a recent brochure issued by The Law Society of England and Wales.[17] This brochure contains nothing less than propaganda for the English legal system, only to entice foreigners to make English law the applicable law (and to choose, in commercial matters, London as the place of arbitration). The brochure lists the reasons why English law should be preferred, advertising English law as, 'more flexible than many civil law systems.' This led to a reaction by the German Ministry of Justice that issued its own pamphlet called 'Law – Made in Germany: global, effective and cost-efficient.'[18] This document markets German law as the best jurisdiction in the world. The existence of both brochures seems to suggest that law has become a sexy product that has to be sold.

What should we think of these four phenomena? It may be that they are known individually, but it is seldom realised that, when taken together, they tell us something about the future of national law. It is beyond doubt that national law still exists and the national legislature may continue to have the Westphalian ambition to set the law for its citizens. However, in reality this national law is surpassed: it is not only replaced by activities of other institutions, it is also increasingly evaded by private actors themselves. One is tempted to say that State authority is leaking away: upwards (to the supranational and European institutions), sideways (to agencies and the law of other States) and downwards (to the citizens themselves).[19] I admit that looking at law in this way presupposes a different view of law than the one that States like best: they will insist that the truly important rules should have passed the national Parliaments. My view is different: if one looks at rules as setting rights

17 Available at <http://www.lawsociety.org.uk>.
18 Available at <http://www.lawmadeingermany.de>.
19 Cutler, *o.c.*, at 51.

and obligations for the parties, one cannot deny that the emergence of such rules is now dependent on many more things other than only the national institutions.

And yet, we continue to think of law as primarily a national phenomenon, with only some international aspects here and there. This prevailing view could be called Private Law+. In Private Law+, the four phenomena which I just described are not internalised, they are only seen as supplementing the existing law. I think this is wrong. If we accept that the State no longer has a monopoly in lawmaking, and therefore take seriously the plurality of sources I just described, we should also think through the consequences this has for our view of law. In other words: instead of Private Law+, we need Private law 2.0. This is just another application in the field of private law of the decline of the nation-state in general, a turn away from what Weiler once qualified as a 'polity based on the tired old ideas of an ethno-culturally homogeneous Volk and the unholy Trinity of *Volk-Staat-Staatsangehöriger*'.[20]

20 J.H.H. Weiler, Does Europe need a Constitution? Demos, Telos and the German Maastricht Decision, *European Law Journal* 1 (1995), 219 ff., at 223.

Private Law 2.0: On the Functions of Codification

The above considerations have brought us right into the heart of the research programme of The Hague Institute on the Internationalisation of Law. The research of HiiL is focused on the question of what is the role of national law in a global society. The answer to this question is relatively easy when it comes to a factual description: compared to what it once was, national law has undoubtedly become less important. However, much more difficult to assess is what we can conclude from this in relation to the role that national law *should* play in a post-national society. The second part of this lecture is devoted to this more normative question. It would be impossible to discuss this question in much detail, but I do wish to show you what is, in my view, the most fruitful approach in dealing with the challenges that post-national law poses. To this end, I propose a functional approach: if we want to develop a Private law 2.0, a promising research method is to look into the functions that present day private law aims to serve, and then see how these functions are perhaps better fulfilled in a different way in a post-national society. I will apply this approach to what can be seen as the central institution of the civil law: the Civil Code.

Following the classical distinction by Maillet,[21] three different functions of codification can be distinguished. They offer insight into the fundamental question of why one would like to lay down the law in a comprehensive set of rules that is issued by the State. Although the functions Maillet identifies are particularly important to understand the coming into being of European codifications in the nineteenth century, they are also useful in understanding the present efforts to codify the existing law.

21 Jean Maillet, The Historical Significance of French Codifications, *Tulane Law Review* 44 (1969-1970), 681 ff. Cf. Jürgen Basedow, Transjurisdictional Codification, *Tulane Law Review* 83 (2008-2009), 973 ff. This does of course not mean that codification could not also have other functions.

The first function of codification is to expose the law, so as to present the existing or desired law in a comprehensive, rational and systematic way. The reason behind this aim is undoubtedly to enhance the accessibility and predictability of the law, telling private actors what their rights and obligations are. When Jeremy Bentham famously wrote 'a complete digest: such is the first rule. Whatever is not in the code of laws, ought not to be law. Nothing ought to be referred either to custom, or to foreign law, or to pretended natural law, or to pretended laws of nations',[22] he exactly sought to remedy the fact that law, in his time, was not accessible to everyone. In a letter to the American President James Madison, he even uses a term that is very familiar to continental lawyers, namely the term 'cognoscibility', being capable of knowing.[23] Promoting this cognoscibility of the law was also one of the main reasons behind the enactment of the Code Napoleon. This is clearly visible if one visits Napoleon's tomb in the Dôme des Invalides in Paris, where the ornament devoted to the Code Civil emphasises both the 'simplicité' of the Code and the fact that the law had now finally become 'intelligible pour tous'. But also today, this motive is still important: when the Dutch enacted the main part of their new Civil Code in 1992, one of the main reasons for this was to make the whole of Dutch private law consistent again.[24] Furthermore, the present debate about the future of European contract law is primarily initiated by the concern of the European Commission that the present *acquis* is too fragmentary and therefore needs to be reorganised in a more coherent way.[25]

The second function of codification is, at least historically, to unify the law. This unification aimed to achieve two different things. On the one hand, codification often sought to eliminate territorial diversity, abolishing diverging laws within one country. The main reason for this type of unification is to serve the economic good: unification of law would promote trade. This

22 Jeremy Bentham, A General View of a Complete Code of Laws, 1802, in: John Bowring (ed.), *The Works of Jeremy Bentham*, vol. III, Edinburgh 1839, 155 ff., at 205.

23 Jeremy Bentham, 1811, in: John Bowring (ed.), *The Works of Jeremy Bentham,* vol. IV, Edinburgh 1843, at 454.

24 Cf. J.H.A. Lokin & W.J. Zwalve, *Hoofdstukken uit de Europese codificatiegeschiedenis*, 3th ed., Den Haag 2006.

25 This motive can already be found in the first Communication (...) on European Contract Law, COM (2001) 398 final. See most recently the Green Paper from the Commission on policy options for progress towards a European contract law for consumers and businesses, COM (2010) 348 final.

motive cannot only be seen in the codifications of the nineteenth century, it is still used today. The European Commission uses the same motive when it spells out the need for a more uniform contract law to enhance the European economy – no doubt prompted to do so by the only limited competence of Art. 114 of the Treaty on the Functioning of the European Union. The recently published draft for a comprehensive codification of Chinese private law adopts the same position: it states that the present situation in China is not ideal: separate regulations on General Principles of Civil Law, Contract Law, Law of Real Rights, Marriage Law, Adoption Law and Inheritance Law would lead to coordination problems that are supposed to endanger the needs of the market economy, in particular on a more and more unified national market.[26] On the other hand, codification in the past also served to unify the status of people. In particular the Code Napoleon explicitly aimed to create equality among citizens by abolishing existing privileges for the nobility and clergy (which is the reason why the Code Civil is sometimes described as the true constitution of France[27]).

The third (historical) function of codification laid in the desire of the national legislature to modify the nature of the law itself: the prevailing laws were no longer to be based on custom (as in feudal law), on foreign law (such as Roman law), on religious law (such as Canon law) or on 'pretended natural law' (as Bentham called it). Instead, law became the product of the nation-state and therefore a democratic thing. The main concern here was one of legitimacy: by requiring that law would pass through the national parliaments, the citizens who were subject to the prevailing rules also became their authors.

26 Liang Huixing (ed.), *The Draft Civil Code of the People's Republic of China: English Translation*, Leiden 2010, Preface.

27 The reference is to Jean Carbonnier, *Droit civil: Introduction*, 20th ed., Paris 1991, 123: 'le Code civil reste la constitution la plus authentique du pays'.

It is clear that these three functions still play a role today when States decide to codify their law. However, one can very well question whether each of these functions is still met in the best possible way by making use of the instrument of codification, either at the national or at the European level. I applied a functional approach to the second[28] and the third[29] function of codification in previous work and I will now focus on the first one: can the function of keeping the law intelligible still be satisfied by codification in our present globalised society? I believe to have shown in the first part of this lecture that this is not the case: law today flows from too many sources.

This prompts the need to think about an alternative. In my view, this alternative cannot lie in what may be the natural reaction of States when confronted with a globalising society: to try to regain what they lost. States can after all try to *domesticate* the new types of rules that were mentioned in the first part of this lecture. A similar reaction would be to argue in favour of a European Civil Code, or even to propose regulation at a global level – as we saw when the financial crisis broke out. In my view these inherited ways of thinking are doomed to failure: in a post-national society, the traditional lawgivers can no longer fulfil the functions of codification I just described. And this may of course not only be true for private law, but also for other traditional legal fields. Recognising this is essential: Stateness is still everywhere in analysing our law, even though the State is on the retreat.[30] In the third part of this lecture, I will have a look at the three different actors that can help in designing private law in a different way: private actors (citizens and firms), legislators and professors.[31]

28 See Jan Smits (ed.), *The Need for a European Contract Law: Empirical and Legal Perspectives*, Groningen 2005. Cf. Gary Low, How and Why we are (not) bothered by the Costs of Legal Diversity: A Behavioural Approach to the Harmonization of European Contract Law, *European Review of Private Law* 18 (2010), 285 ff.

29 See Jan Smits, Democracy and (European) Private Law: A Functional Approach, *European Journal of Legal Studies* 2 (2009), 26 ff.

30 Cf. For a similar view in the field of constitutional law: René Barents, The Precedence of EU Law from the Perspective of Constitutional Pluralism, *European Constitutional Law Review* 5 (2009), 421 ff., at 441 referring to misleading 'state-centred thinking.'

31 The allusion is, of course, to R.C. van Caenegem, *Judges, Legislators and Professors*, Cambridge 1987.

Private Actors, Legislators and Professors

The gist of the above is that it is wrong to make the State uniquely responsible for deciding which law is to apply to its citizens. Instead, the citizens themselves should play an important role in deciding which law applies to (at least part of) their activities. This fits in with the view that the present vacuum in global regulation (the traditional suppliers of law fail to regulate things at the global level) should make the demand side more important. This demand side consists of the end-users of law, so private actors such as consumers and firms. Within the limits set by mandatory law, they should be able to choose a legal system that in their view fits in best with the type of activity they engage in. The prerequisite then is that the end-users of law are not forced to 'buy' the entire bundle of public goods of one particular country, but are able to differentiate. As O'Hara and Ribstein recently argued, relating to the American situation, people should be able to choose the law that best suits a part of their lives, for example, incorporate their corporation in Delaware, conclude their contracts according to the law of the state of New York and live in California.[32] This means one is no longer governed by one law for everything that one does. Taking this view seriously means that the role of private actors will fundamentally change. From being subjected to one indivisible national law through a fictitious social contract, we are moving towards a situation in which citizens choose those segments of different jurisdictions they like best. Some authors have put this idea to extremes, claiming for example that even citizenship should be at the free choice of people.[33]

I do not deny that parties may also be tempted to find the certainty they need not in law (by choosing other jurisdictions), but in non-legal devices. Much of private law is about creating trust among parties and there are other ways to realise this than by relying on legal rules.

32 On the idea of people as buyers of law, see O'Hara & Ribstein, *o.c.*, 14 ff.

33 See *e.g.* Bruno S. Frey & Reiner Eichenberger, *The New Democratic Federalism for Europe*, Northampton 1999.

34 Omri Ben-Shahar, The Myth of the 'Opportunity to Read' in Contract Law, *European Review of Contract Law* 5 (2008), 1 ff.

In particular so-called indicators of reputation can play an important role: just as websites such as booking.com inform consumers about the quality of hotels based on reviews of previous guests, and ratings on eBay tell potential sellers and buyers about the reliability of future counterparts, similar rating and labelling mechanisms can be put into place for contract law in general.[34] These mechanisms replace enforcement of rules by the State *afterwards* (in case things went wrong) for parties relying on reputation indicators *before* entering into a contract. Certainty is then not sought in law, but the law *itself* is replaced by other mechanisms. Although this is an important phenomenon that needs to be looked at more often, I will not pay any further attention to it in this lecture.

The view of citizens choosing segments of different jurisdictions raises many questions of both a theoretical and a practical nature. The question I like to mention today is how private actors know which options to choose from. Here, they have little to expect from the national legislators, who will invariably promote their own national law and remain silent about the possibility to choose another jurisdiction. This is not a problem for large multinational companies or for wealthy individuals, who are able to get the legal advice they need at whatever price is asked. However, the situation is different for citizens like Samantha, who often do not know about the very possibility of choosing another legal regime, let alone about the benefits and disadvantages of the options that exist. As we saw before, Jeremy Bentham's concern in the late eighteenth century was that the law was only accessible for a small group of people. As a result of increasing internationalisation, normal citizens are today just as ignorant of the possibilities the law offers them to shape their own lives as the people that Bentham lamented. In this respect, we are back in the time of before the great nineteenth century codifications, a time in which it greatly mattered for the law what was one's status in society. I suggest that we do away with this inequality among people by giving more and better information on the existing legal regimes and the extent to which people can choose among them. One possibility would be to create, by way of private initiative, a website on which the benefits and disadvantages are sketched of the various legal segments that private actors can choose. Such comparison sites already exist for many consumer products. The website would depict clickable icons in fields as diverse as marriage, succession, mortgage, adoption, formation of contract, citizenship and incorporation of a company, allowing private actors to build their own personalised legal system.

The second type of actor is the legislator. What role should legislators play in a post-national society? The obvious answer is that they have to set the limits for choice. They should take care of protecting weaker parties, such as consumers and employees, by providing mandatory law from which one cannot deviate. No doubt this is a role for the national and European legislator: identifying the exact limits of party choice is a vital component of an approach that emphasises the importance of people choosing their own laws.[35] At the same time, it is surprising that present-day legislators are not more creative than just doing this. To them, rules are either mandatory or facilitative, with often only very little in between. As we saw, this no longer fits the needs of parties that have become much more individualised in today's society. This could even be the very reason why people start shopping elsewhere for their law. The rhetorical question is whether the national legislator should not also give its own citizens more options, thus making national law more attractive again. At the moment, legislators seem obsessed by a quest for coherence, meaning that there can be only one rule on a certain issue. They then forget that the function of coherence is to make the law predictable and that

35 This also implies a shift away from 'traditional egalitarian conceptions of justice requiring uniform treatment for everyone' towards guaranteeing basic minimum rights and combating poverty and insecurity: see Veit Bader, Building European Institutions: Beyond Strong Ties and Weak Commitments, in: Seyla Benhabib et al (eds.), *Identities, Affiliations and Allegiances*, Cambridge 2007, at 132.

achieving this goal is not incompatible with giving people the freedom to choose from a limited menu of options. In my view, supported by economic analysis, such options can in some cases even replace mandatory law.[36] If a consumer buys a product over the internet, it is allowed to send it back to the seller within seven working days after delivery.[37] Would it not be nice if the consumer would alternatively have the right to purchase the item without this right of withdrawal, but then at a lower price? It would enable people to decide for themselves whether they prefer to have the extra protection or simply pay less. This would provide citizens with an option between two different mandatory regimes.[38]

The European legislature already discovered the attractiveness of optional regimes. It created several sets of optional law as so-called 28th European legal systems, next to the national laws. Private actors can decide for themselves whether they want to opt in to these sets of rules or stick to their national law (or choose the law of a third country). The European Company (SE) is one popular example of this phenomenon: more than 200 companies already registered as an SE, including multinationals like BASF and Porsche. In the near future, we will most likely not only have a European Private Company (SPE), but also a 28th optional European contract law. These examples of optional law[39] at the European level deserve to be followed by national legislatures.

Finally, I would like to mention law professors as important actors in a post-national society. It is no secret that I am a fierce believer in an international legal education.[40] The possibility to teach in the European Law School at this University is one of the reasons why I returned to Maastricht. It is a stimulating and exciting experience to participate in this unique programme that attracts students from all over the European Union. But today I did not speak about training European lawyers for

36 See for a general account of the benefits of optional law Gregor Bachmann, Optionsmodelle im Privatrecht, *JuristenZeitung* 63 (2008), 11 ff.

37 Art. 6 Directive 97/7 on distance contracts, *OJ* L 144/19.

38 See Gerhard Wagner, Mandatory Contract Law: Functions and Principles in Light of the Proposal for a Directive on Consumer Rights, *Erasmus Law Review* 3 (2010), 68 ff.

39 Cf. J.M. Smits, Europees recht als alternatief: de charme van het 28ste rechtsstelsel, *Tijdschrift voor Privaatrecht* 46 (2009), 1731 ff.

40 My position is made explicit in Jan M. Smits, European Legal Education, or: How to Prepare Students for Global Citizenship? (forthcoming, 2011).

an international legal career. The real question is what are the consequences of my lecture for the teaching of national law, not only of Dutch law at Dutch law faculties, but also of German law in Germany or of Finnish law in Finland. It is sometimes asserted that studying such a national law would not involve paying attention to how things are elsewhere because practice would not require it. Here, I wholeheartedly disagree. Even if it were true that the only aim of studying, *e.g.*, Dutch law is to offer a specialised professional training in becoming a lawyer – something I would deny because I believe students should learn to use the law not only as an instrument, but also to think about law in an intellectual way[41] – we do a bad job if we only teach the law of the State. If the aim of such a professional training is to teach students which rules (can) apply in the Netherlands, allowing them to advise people like Samantha, it is clear that Dutch law itself is only one aspect of this. We are misleading students if we claim otherwise.[42] This calls for an ambitious change of programmes of Dutch law. To end with another rhetorical question: if universities do not take up this challenge to provide intellectual leadership, who will?

With that, it is time to conclude. I have given you a snapshot view of what increasing de-nationalisation means in the field of private law and how the roles of private actors, legislators and universities can be redefined to meet new challenges. Although the format of this lecture did not allow me to go into details, I hope it does give you some idea of the type of work I will do on the Maastricht-HiiL Chair in this academic year. As part of my activities on this Chair, I hope to be able to write a book in which several of the ideas mentioned above will be worked out.

41 Cf. Martha Nussbaum, Cultivating Humanity in Legal Education, *University of Chicago Law Review* 70 (2003), 265 ff.

42 Cf. Mathias Reimann, Beyond national systems, *Tulane Law Review* 75 (2001), 1113 ff.

Words of Thanks

Ladies and Gentlemen, at the end of this inaugural lecture I would like to thank you all for coming here: it means a lot to me. I would like to mention several people in particular.

First of all, these are the people that the university is for: students. It gives me great pleasure that some of you are present here today. I tremendously look forward to exploring the consequences of de-nationalisation of law in the course that I will teach in the context of the Maastricht-HiiL Chair and the MARBLE project. You will find that in my teaching model we search together for answers to the many questions internationalisation of law raises. Your contribution to this search for knowledge is just as important as mine, thus building the micro academic community that I like so much.

I thank the Board of Maastricht University and The Hague Institute on the Internationalisation of Law for having appointed me to this Chair. At HiiL, I thank in particular Sam Muller, David Raic and Laura Kistemaker. I realise it is not self-evident to appoint someone of Dutch nationality to this Chair and I am proud to be this year's Chairholder. I have been involved in HiiL's activities from the very start and it is impressive to see what you have established in only five years time.

This inaugural is for the Maastricht-HiiL Chair, but for me it is also a return to Maastricht and to the Chair of European Private Law. One sometimes needs to leave a place to realise its enormous achievements and potential. Looking at Maastricht from a distance, as I did in the last three years, I saw a Faculty that is truly European, in which people work incredibly hard to achieve common goals, in which there is a sphere of conviviality, and in which strict separations among the legal fields do not exist. Anyone who is interested in a truly international and ambitious legal education would like to study and work at such a Faculty. I thank my colleagues for welcoming me back and in particular I thank the Dean, Aalt Willem Heringa, for his warm welcome and for his great efforts to make it possible that almost the entire TICOM-team could move to Maastricht.

It is a true pleasure to see several colleagues from Tilburg here today. I mention in particular José Sintnicolaas, with whom I worked so pleasantly together in the last three years, and Jan Vranken. Jan, your academic work and your view of what a university is for have always been a source of inspiration to me. Earlier this year in Tilburg, I said that my way of doing research could perhaps be defined as 'not to defend, but to be accused.' The insight that this is a valuable way of doing academic work I owe to you and to Herman Schoordijk. For this, and for many other things, I am most grateful to you. Leaving Tilburg was not an easy decision to make.

I regard the Maastricht Faculty of Law as a whole as my new academic home. However, next to the Department of Private Law, my home in the narrower sense of the word is *M*-EPLI, the Maastricht European Private Law Institute. Upon my arrival, only two months ago, I was pleasantly struck by the enthusiasm that I found with many colleagues for this new initiative. One of the things I like about *M*-EPLI is that people from different backgrounds participate in it, cutting through the departmental structure. This is in my view exactly what universities should encourage: to organise faculties in such a way that research across the various legal fields is promoted. Everyone involved in *M*-EPLI is determined to make it a true academic community, thus combining high-level academic work with the daily joy of working in Maastricht.

De laatste woorden zijn voor Christa. Jij bent de allerbelangrijkste in mijn leven. Als het grootste geluk beschouw ik dat er elke dag momenten zijn waarop ik dat tegen je kan zeggen.

Ik heb gezegd.

9 789490 947170